The jumblies and other nonsense verses

Edward Lear, L Leslie 1862-1940 Brooke

BOOKS
with Drawings by
LESLIE BROOKE

〜

JOHNNY CROW'S GARDEN

JOHNNY CROW'S PARTY

THE GOLDEN GOOSE BOOK
  The Three Little Pigs
  Tom Thumb
  The Golden Goose
  The Three Bears

RING O' ROSES
  Oranges and Lemons
  The Man in the Moon
  Little Bo-Peep
  This Little Pig went to Market

THE HOUSE IN THE WOOD

THE NURSERY RHYME BOOK
  Edited by Andrew Lang

NONSENSE SONGS
  By Edward Lear

THE TAILOR AND THE CROW

A ROUNDABOUT TURN
  By Robert H Charles

Published by
FREDERICK WARNE & CO LTD

THE JUMBLIES

AND

OTHER NONSENSE VERSES.

PRINTED IN GREAT BRITAIN

THE JUMBLIES

AND OTHER NONSENSE VERSES BY
EDWARD LEAR
AUTHOR OF 'THE BOOK OF NONSENSE'

WITH DRAWINGS BY
L·LESLIE BROOKE

FREDERICK WARNE AND CO LD
LONDON   NEW YORK

C 951941

INTRODUCTORY.

———•———

ENCOURAGED by the cordial reception extended by
Press and Public to their issue of the " Pelican Chorus
and Other Nonsense Verses by Edward Lear," newly
illustrated, the Publishers have requested the Artist, Mr.
L. Leslie Brooke, to do a similar service for a further selection
from Lear's Nonsense Songs, thus practically completing them.
In addition to "The Jumblies," which has been adopted as the
titular piece, this volume includes such prime favourites as
"The Owl and the Pussy Cat," "The Duck and the Kangaroo,"
and "The Dong with a Luminous Nose" For the benefit of
those whose memories of the Nonsense Songs are not as fresh
as they should be, it may be repeated that Mr. Lear did not
illustrate them as fully as was his custom; some, indeed, had
no drawings at all, and others merely a headpiece. The
Publishers feel, therefore, that in re-issuing the songs adequately
illustrated, they are but bringing them into line with Mr. Lear's
other works.

Oliver Wendell Holmes, has said, in a well-known poem,
that—

> " There is nothing that keeps its youth—
> So far as I know —but a tree and truth "

He might have added certain writings, and among those that
are as fresh to-day as when they were written are the Nonsense
Books of Edward Lear Several generations of children—old
as well as young—have already "drunk delight" from them,

and it is tolerably safe to prophesy that many editions will yet be demanded. But whatever new form the changing public taste may cause them to take, they will remain as fresh to the end as they are to-day. It was one of these books that John Ruskin declared to be "the most beneficent and innocent of all books yet produced." And of the author he said : " I really don't know any author to whom I am half so grateful for my idle self as Edward Lear." This is very high praise from such a source , and in the hope that similar pleasure may be given to many new readers this new edition of the Nonsense Songs is issued.

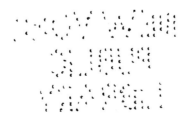

CONTENTS.

———•———

THE JUMBLES.

I.

THEY went to sea in a Sieve, they did,
In a Sieve they went to sea:
In spite of all their friends could say,
On a winter's morn, on a stormy day,
In a Sieve they went to sea!
And when the Sieve turned round and round,
And everyone cried, "You'll all be drowned!"
They cried aloud, "Our Sieve ain't big,
But we don't care a button, we don't care a fig!
In a Sieve we'll go to sea!"

The Jumblies.

Far and few, far and few,
   Are the lands where the Jumblies live;
Their heads are green, and their hands are blue,
   And they went to sea in a Sieve.

II.

They sailed away in a Sieve, they did,
   In a Sieve they sailed so fast,
With only a beautiful pea-green veil
Tied with a riband, by way of a sail,
   To a small tobacco-pipe mast;
And every one said, who saw them go,
"O won't they be soon upset, you know!
For the sky is dark, and the voyage is long,
And happen what may, it's extremely wrong
   In a Sieve to sail so fast!"
      Far and few, far and few,
         Are the lands where the Jumblies live;
Their heads are green, and their hands are blue,
         And they went to sea in a Sieve.

III.

The water it soon came in, it did,
   The water it soon came in;
So to keep them dry, they wrapped their feet
In a pinky paper all folded neat,

And they fastened it down with a pin.
And they passed the night in a crockery-jar,
And each of them said, "How wise we are!
Though the sky be dark, and the voyage be long,
Yet we never can think we were rash or wrong,
    While round in our Sieve we spin!"
        Far and few, far and few,
            Are the lands where the Jumblies live;
        Their heads are green, and their hands are blue,
            And they went to sea in a Sieve.

IV.

And all night long they sailed away;
    And when the sun went down,
They whistled and warbled a moony song
To the echoing sound of a coppery gong,
    In the shade of the mountains brown.
"O Timballo! How happy we are,
When we live in a Sieve and a crockery-jar,
And all night long in the moonlight pale,
We sail away with a pea-green sail,
    In the shade of the mountains brown!"
        Far and few, far and few,
            Are the lands where the Jumblies live;
        Their heads are green, and their hands are blue,
            And they went to sea in a Sieve.

V.

They sailed to the Western sea, they did,
To a land all covered with trees,

And they bought an Owl, and a useful Cart,
And a pound of Rice, and a Cranberry Tart,
   And a hive of silvery Bees.
And they bought a Pig, and some green Jack-daws,
And a lovely Monkey with lollipop paws,
And forty bottles of Ring-Bo-Ree,
   And no end of Stilton Cheese.
     Far and few, far and few,
       Are the lands where the Jumblies live;

Their heads are green, and their hands are blue,
And they went to sea in a Sieve.

VI.

And in twenty years they all came back,
In twenty years or more,
And every one said, "How tall they've grown!
For they've been to the Lakes, and the Terrible Zone,
And the hills of the Chankly Bore;"
And they drank their health, and gave them a feast
Of dumplings made of beautiful yeast;
And every one said, "If we only live,
We too will go to sea in a Sieve—
To the hills of the Chankly Bore!"
Far and few, far and few,
Are the lands where the Jumblies live;
Their heads are green, and their hands are blue,
And they went to sea in a Sieve

The Owl and the Pussy-Cat

THE OWL AND THE PUSSY-CAT.

I.

THE Owl and the Pussy-Cat went to sea
In a beautiful pea-green boat,
They took some honey, and plenty of money,
Wrapped up in a five-pound note.
The Owl looked up to the stars above,
And sang to a small guitar,
"O lovely Pussy! O Pussy, my love,
What a beautiful Pussy you are,
You are,
You are!
What a beautiful Pussy you are!"

II.

Pussy said to the Owl, "You elegant fowl!
How charmingly sweet you sing!
O let us be married! too long we have tarried:
But what shall we do for a ring?"

They sailed away for a year and a day,
 To the land where the Bong-tree grows,
And there in a wood a Piggy-wig stood,
 With a ring at the end of his nose.
   His nose,
   His nose,
With a ring at the end of his nose.

III.

"Dear Pig, are you willing to sell for one shilling
  Your ring?" Said the Piggy, "I will."
So they took it away, and were married next day
  By the Turkey who lives on the hill.
They dinèd on mince, and slices of quince,
  Which they ate with a runcible spoon;
And hand in hand, on the edge of the sand,
  They danced by the light of the moon,
      The moon,
      The moon,
They danced by the light of the moon.

THE BROOM, THE SHOVEL, THE POKER AND THE TONGS.

I.

THE Broom and the Shovel, the Poker and Tongs,
  They all took a drive in the Park,
    And they each sang a song, Ding-a-dong!
      Ding-a-dong!
Before they went back in the dark.
Mr. Poker he sat quite upright in the coach,
  Mr. Tongs made a clatter and clash,
Miss Shovel was dressed all in black (with a brooch),
  Mrs. Broom was in blue (with a sash).
    Ding-a-dong! Ding-a-dong!
    And they all sang a song!

II.

"O Shovely so lovely!" the Poker he sang,
  "You have perfectly conquered my heart!
" Ding-a-dong! Ding-a-dong! If you're pleased with
  my song

'I will feed you with cold apple tart!
'When you scrape up the coals with a delicate sound,
"You enrapture my life with delight!
"Your nose is so shiny! your head is so round!
"And your shape is so slender and bright!
"Ding-a-dong! Ding-a-dong!
"Ain't you pleased with my song?"

III.

"Alas! Mrs. Broom!" sighed the Tongs in his song,
"O is it because I'm so thin,
"And my legs are so long—Ding-a-dong! Ding-a-
dong!
"That you don't care about me a pin?
"Ah! fairest of creatures, when sweeping the room,
"Ah! why don't you heed my complaint?
"Must you needs be so cruel, you beautiful Broom,
"Because you are covered with paint?
"Ding-a-dong! Ding-a-dong!
"You are certainly wrong!"

IV.

Mrs. Broom and Miss Shovel together they sang,
"What nonsense you're singing to-day!"
Said the Shovel, "I'll certainly hit you a bang!"
Said the Broom, "And I'll sweep you away!"

The Broom, the Shovel, the Poker and the Tongs.

So the Coachman drove homeward as fast as he could,
   Perceiving their anger with pain;
But they put on the kettle, and little by little
   They all became happy again.
      Ding-a-dong! Ding-a-dong!
      There's an end of my song!

The Duck and the Kangaroo

THE DUCK AND THE KANGAROO.

I.

SAID the Duck to the Kangaroo,
　　"Good gracious! how you hop!
　　Over the fields and the water too,
　As if you never would stop!
My life is a bore in this nasty pond,
And I long to go out in the world beyond!

The Duck and the Kangaroo.

I wish I could hop like you!"
Said the Duck to the Kangaroo.

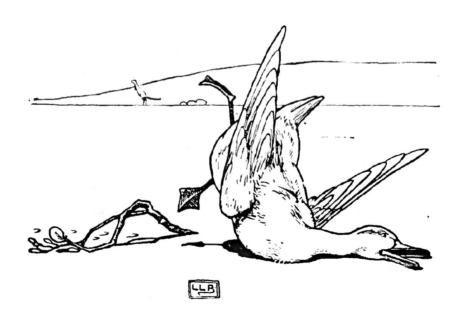

II.

" Please give me a ride on your back ! "
   Said the Duck to the Kangaroo.
" I would sit quite still, and say nothing but ' Quack,'
   The whole of the long day through !
And we'd go to the Dee, and the Jelly Bo Lee,
Over the land, and over the sea ;—
   Please take me a ride ! O do ! "
   Said the Duck to the Kangaroo.

III.

Said the Kangaroo to the Duck,
   " This requires some little reflection :
Perhaps on the whole it might bring me luck,
   And there seems but one objection,
Which is, if you'll let me speak so bold,
Your feet are unpleasantly wet and cold,
   And would probably give me the roo-
   Matiz ! " said the Kangaroo.

IV.

Said the Duck, " As I sat on the rocks,
   I have thought over that completely,
And I bought four pairs of worsted socks
   Which fit my web-feet neatly.

The Duck and the Kangaroo.

And to keep out the cold I've bought a cloak,
And every day a cigar I'll smoke,
    All to follow my own dear true
    Love of a Kangaroo!"

V.

Said the Kangaroo, " I'm ready !
  All in the moonlight pale ;
But to balance me well, dear Duck, sit steady !
  And quite at the end of my tail ! "
So away they went with a hop and a bound,
And they hopped the whole world three times round ;
  And who so happy,—O who,
  As the Duck and the Kangaroo ?

THE CUMMERBUND.

AN INDIAN POEM.

SHE sat upon her Dobie,[1]
    To watch the Evening Star,
      And all the Punkahs[2] as they passed
    Cried, "My! how fair you are!"
Around her bower, with quivering leaves,
    The tall Kamsamahs[3] grew,

[1] *Washerman.*

[2] *Fan.*

[3] *Butler.*

And Kitmutgars[1] in wild festoons   [1] *Waiter at table.*
    Hung down from Tchokis[2] blue. [2] *Police or post station.*

II.

Below her home the river rolled
    With soft meloobious sound,
Where golden-finned Chuprassies[3] swam,
    In myriads circling round.   [3] *Office messenger.*
Above, on tallest trees remote,
    Green Ayahs perched alone,
And all night long the Mussak[4] moaned   [4] *Water skin.*
    Its melancholy tone.

III.

And where the purple Nullahs[5] threw   [5] *Watercourse.*
    Their branches far and wide,
And silvery Goreewallahs[6] flew   [6] *Groom.*
    In silence, side by side,
The little Bheesties'[7] twittering cry   [7] *Water-carrier.*
    Rose on the fragrant air,
And oft the angry Jampan[8] howled   [8] *Sedan Chair.*
    Deep in his hateful lair.

IV.

She sat upon her Dobie,—
    She heard the Nimmak[9] hum,—   [9] *Salt.*
When all at once a cry arose:
    "The Cummerbund[10] is come!"   [10] *Waist sash.*

In vain she fled ;—with open jaws
  The angry monster followed,
And so (before assistance came),
  That Lady Fair was swallowed.

V.

They sought in vain for even a bone
  Respectfully to bury ;
They said, " Hers was a dreadful fate ! "
  (And Echo answered, " Very.")
They nailed her Dobie to the wall,
  Where last her form was seen,
And underneath they wrote these words.
  In yellow, blue, and green :—
" Beware, ye Fair ! Ye Fair, beware !
  Nor sit out late at night,
Lest horrid Cummerbunds should come,
  And swallow you outright."

NOTE.—First published in the *Times of India*, Bombay, July, 1874.

THE DONG WITH A LUMINOUS NOSE.

WHEN awful darkness and silence reign
    Over the great Gromboolian plain,
      Through the long, long wintry nights;—
When the angry breakers roar,
As they beat on the rocky shore;—
    When Storm-clouds brood on the towering
      heights
Of the Hills on the Chankly Bore:—

Then, through the vast and gloomy dark,
There moves what seems a fiery spark,
    A lonely spark with silvery rays
    Piercing the coal-black night.—
    A meteor strange and bright:—

The Dong with a Luminous Nose.

Hither and thither the vision strays,
    A single lurid light.

Slowly it wanders,—pauses,—creeps,—
Anon it sparkles,—flashes and leaps;
And ever as onward it gleaming goes
A light on the Bong-tree stems it throws.
And those who watch at that midnight hour
From Hall or Terrace, or lofty Tower,
Cry, as the wild light passes along,—
        "The Dong!—the Dong!
    "The wandering Dong through the forest goes!
        "The Dong! the Dong!
    "The Dong with a luminous Nose!"

        Long years ago
    The Dong was happy and gay,
Till he fell in love with a Jumbly Girl
    Who came to those shores one day.
For the Jumblies came in a Sieve, they did,—
Landing at eve near the Zemmery Fidd
        Where the Oblong Oysters grow,
    And the rocks are smooth and gray.
And all the woods and the valleys rang
With the Chorus they daily and nightly sang,—

The Dong with a Luminous Nose.

" Far and few, far and few,
Are the lands where the Jumblies live;
Their heads are green, and their hands are blue,
And they went to sea in a Sieve."

Happily, happily passed those days!
    While the cheerful Jumblies staid;
They danced in circlets all night long,
To the plaintive pipe of the lively Dong,
    In moonlight, shine, or shade,
For day and night he was always there
By the side of the **Jumbly Girl** so fair,
With her sky-blue hands, and her sea-green hair.

The Dong with a Luminous Nose.

Till the morning came of that hateful day
When the Jumblies sailed in their Sieve away,
And the Dong was left on the cruel shore
Gazing—gazing for evermore,—
Ever keeping his weary eyes on
That pea-green sail on the far horizon,—
Singing the Jumbly Chorus still
As he sat all day on the grassy hill,—

> " *Far and few, far and few,*
>   *Are the lands where the Jumblies live ;*
>   *Their heads are green, and their hands are blue,*
>   *And they went to sea in a Sieve.*"

The Dong with a Luminous Nose.

But when the sun was low in the West,
  The Dong arose and said,—
  "What little sense I once possessed
  Has quite gone out of my head!"

The Dong with a Luminous Nose.

And since that day he wanders still
By lake and forest, marsh and hill,
Singing—" O somewhere, in valley or plain
"Might I find my Jumbly Girl again !
"For ever I'll seek by lake and shore
'Till I find my Jumbly Girl once more !"
Playing a pipe with silvery squeaks,
Since then his Jumbly Girl he seeks,
And because by night he could not see,
He gathered the bark of the Twangum Tree
On the flowery plain that grows.
And he wove him a wondrous Nose,—
A Nose as strange as a Nose could be !
Of vast proportions and painted red,
And tied with cords to the back of his head.
—In a hollow rounded space it ended
With a luminous lamp within suspended,
All fenced about
With a bandage stout
To prevent the wind from blowing
it out ;—
And with holes all round to send the light,
In gleaming rays on the dismal night.

And now each night, and all night long,
Over those plains still roams the Dong !

And above the wail of the Chimp and Snipe
You may hear the squeak of his plaintive pipe,
While ever he seeks, but seeks in vain,
To meet with his Jumbly Girl again;
Lonely and wild—all night he goes,—
The Dong with a luminous Nose!
And all who watch at the midnight hour,
From Hall or Terrace, or Lofty Tower,
Cry, as they trace the Meteor bright,
Moving along through the dreary night,—

      "This is the hour when forth he goes,
      "The Dong with a luminous Nose!
      " Yonder—over the plain he goes;
        " He goes ;
        " He goes !
     "The Dong with a luminous Nose!"

THE NEW VESTMENTS.

THERE lived an old man in the Kingdom of Tess,
Who invented a purely original dress ;
And when it was perfectly made and complete,
He opened the door, and walked into the street.

By way of a hat he'd a loaf of Brown Bread,
In the middle of which he inserted his head ;—
His Shirt was made up of no end of dead Mice,
The warmth of whose skins was quite fluffy and nice ;—
His Drawers were of Rabbit-skins ;—so were his Shoes ;—
His Stockings were skins,—but it is not known whose :—
His Waistcoat and Trowsers were made of Pork Chops ;—
His Buttons were Jujubes and Chocolate Drops ;—
His Coat was all Pancakes, with Jam for a border,
And a girdle of Biscuits to keep it in order ;
And he wore over all, as a screen from bad weather,
A Cloak of green Cabbage-leaves stitched all together.

He had walked a short way, when he heard a great noise,
Of all sorts of Beasticles, Birdlings, and Boys ;—

And from every long street and dark lane in the town
Beasts, Birdles, and Boys in a tumult rushed down.
Two Cows and a Calf ate his Cabbage-leaf Cloak;—
Four Apes seized his Girdle, which vanished like smoke;—

The New Vestments.

Three Kids ate up half of his Pancaky Coat,—
And the tails were devoured by an ancient He Goat;—
An army of Dogs in a twinkling tore *up* his
Pork Waistcoat and Trowsers to give to their Puppies;—
And while they were growling, and mumbling the Chops,
Ten Boys prigged the Jujubes and Chocolate Drops.
He tried to run back to his house, but in vain,
For scores of fat Pigs came again and again;—
They rushed out of stables and hovels and doors,—
They tore off his Stockings, his Shoes, and his Drawers.
And now from the housetops with screechings descend,
Striped, spotted, white, black, and grey Cats without end;
They jumped on his shoulders and knocked off his Hat,—
When Crows, Ducks and Hens made a mincemeat of
        that :—
They speedily flew at his sleeves in a trice,
And utterly tore up his Shirt of dead Mice;—
They swallowed the last of his Shirt with a squall,—
Whereon he ran home with no clothes on at all.

And he said to himself as he bolted the door,
" I will not wear a similar dress any more,
" Any more, any more, any more, never more '"

Calico
Pie

CALICO PIE.

I.

CALICO Pie,
  The Little Birds fly
    Down to the calico tree,
Their wings were blue,
And they sang "Tilly-loo!"
Till away they flew,—
  And they never came back to me!
    They never came back!

They never came back!
They never came back to me!

ii.

Calico Jam,
The little Fish swam
Over the syllabub sea,
He took off his hat,
To the Sole and the Sprat,
And the Willeby-wat,—
But he never came back to me!
He never came back!
He never came back!
He never came back to me!

iii.

Calico Ban,
The little Mice ran,
To be ready in time for tea,
Flippity flup,
They drank it all up,
And danced in the cup,—
But they never came back to me!
They never came back!
They never came back!
They never came back to me!

IV.

Calico Drum,
The Grasshoppers come,
The Butterfly, Beetle, and Bee,
Over the ground,
Around and around,
With a hop and a bound —
But they never came back!
They never came back!
They never came back!
They never came back to me!

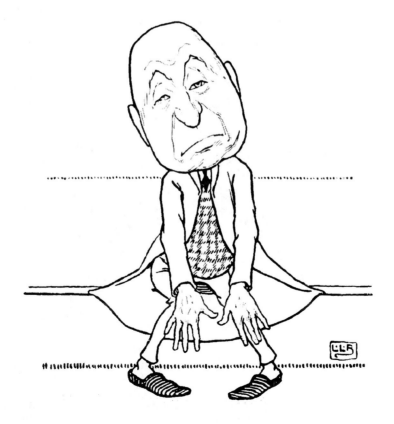

The Courtship of the Yonghy-Bonghy-Bò

THE YONGHY-BONGHY-BÒ.

THE COURTSHIP OF THE YONGHY-BONGHY-BÒ.

I.

ON the Coast of Coromandel,
  Where the early pumpkins grow,
    In the middle of the woods
  Lived the Yonghy-Bonghy-Bò.
Two old chairs, and half a candle,—
One old jug without a handle,—
    These were all his worldly goods:
    In the middle of the woods,
    These were all the worldly goods
  Of the Yonghy-Bonghy-Bò,
  Of the Yonghy-Bonghy-Bò.

II.

Once, among the Bong-trees walking
  Where the early pumpkins grow,
    To a little heap of stones
  Came the Yonghy-Bonghy-Bò.
There he heard a Lady talking,
To some milk-white Hens of Dorking,—
    "'Tis the Lady Jingly Jones!

"On that little heap of stones
"Sits the Lady Jingly Jones!"
Said the Yonghy-Bonghy-Bò,
Said the Yonghy-Bonghy-Bò.

III.

" Lady Jingly! Lady Jingly!
  "Sitting where the pumpkins grow,
    "Will you come and be my wife?"
Said the Yonghy-Bonghy-Bò.
"I am tired of living singly,—
"On this coast so wild and shingly,—
    "I'm a-weary of my life,
    "If you'll come and be my wife,
    "Quite serene would be my life!"—
Said the Yonghy-Bonghy-Bò,
Said the Yonghy-Bonghy-Bò.

IV.

'On this Coast of Coromandel,
  "Shrimps and watercresses grow,
    "Prawns are plentiful and cheap."
Said the Yonghy-Bonghy-Bò.
"You shall have my chairs and candle,
"And my jug without a handle!—
    "Gaze upon the rolling deep
    ("Fish is plentiful and cheap)—
    "As the sea, my love is deep!"

Said the Yonghy-Bonghy-Bò,
Said the Yonghy-Bonghy-Bò.

v.

Lady Jingly answered sadly,
   And her tears began to flow,—
      "Your proposal comes too late,
   " Mr. Yonghy-Bonghy-Bò!
"I would be your wife most gladly!"
(Here she twirled her fingers madly)

"But in England I've a mate!

"Yes! you've asked me far too late,

"For in England I've a mate,

"Mr. Yonghy-Bonghy-Bò!

"Mr. Yonghy-Bonghy-Bò!

VI.

"Mr. Jones—(his name is Handel,—

"Handel Jones, Esquire, & Co.)

"Dorking fowls delights to send,

"Mr. Yonghy-Bonghy-Bò!

"Keep, oh! keep your chairs and candle,

"And your jug without a handle,—

"I can merely be your friend!

"—Should my Jones more Dorkings send,

"I will give you three, my friend!

"Mr. Yonghy-Bonghy-Bò!

"Mr. Yonghy-Bonghy-Bò!

VII.

"Though you've such a tiny body,

"And your head so large doth grow,—

"Though your hat may blow away,

"Mr. Yonghy-Bonghy-Bò!

"Though you're such a Boddy Doddy—

"Yet I wish that I could modi-

"fy the words I needs must say!

"Will you please to go away?

"That is all I have to say—
"Mr. Yonghy-Bonghy-Bò,
"Mr. Yonghy-Bonghy-Bò!"

VIII.

Down the slippery slopes of Myrtle,
    Where the early pumpkins grow,
        To the calm and silent sea
    Fled the Yonghy-Bonghy-Bò.
There beyond the Bay of Gurtle,
Lay a large and lively Turtle;—
        "You're the Cove," he said, "for me;
        "On your back beyond the sea,
        "Turtle, you shall carry me!"

H

Said the Yonghy-Bonghy-Bò.
Said the Yonghy-Bonghy-Bò.

IX.

Through the silent-roaring ocean
Did the Turtle swiftly go;
Holding fast upon his shell
Rode the Yonghy-Bonghy-Bò,
With a sad primæval motion
Towards the sunset isles of Boshen
Still the Turtle bore him well,
Holding fast upon his shell.
"Lady Jingly Jones, farewell!"
Sang the Yonghy-Bonghy-Bò,
Sang the Yonghy-Bonghy-Bò.

X.

From the Coast of Coromandel
Did that Lady never go;
On that heap of stones she mourns
For the Yonghy-Bonghy-Bò.
On that Coast of Coromandel,
In his jug without a handle,
Still she weeps, and daily moans;
On that little heap of stones
To her Dorking Hens she moans
For the Yonghy-Bonghy-Bò,
For the Yonghy-Bonghy-Bò.

INCIDENTS IN THE LIFE OF MY UNCLE ARLY.

———•———

I.

O MY AGED UNCLE ARLY!
 Sitting on a heap of Barley
  Thro' the silent hours of night,—
Close beside a leafy thicket :—
On his nose there was a Cricket,—
In his hat a Railway-Ticket
  (But his shoes were far too tight).

II.

Long ago, in youth, he squander'd
All his goods away, and wander'd
  To the Tiniskoop-hills afar.
There on golden sunsets blazing,
Every evening found him gazing,—
Singing,—"Orb! you're quite amazing!
  "How I wonder what you are!"

III.

Like the ancient Medes and Persians,
Always by his own exertions

He subsisted on those hills;—
Whiles,—by teaching children spelling,—
Or at times by merely yelling,—
Or at intervals by selling
    "Propter's Nicodemus Pills."

IV.

Later, in his morning rambles
He perceived the moving brambles—
    Something square and white disclose :—
'Twas a First-class Railway-Ticket;
But, on stooping down to pick it
Off the ground,—a pea-green Cricket
    Settled on my uncle's Nose.

V.

Never—never more,—oh! never,
Did that Cricket leave him ever,—
    Dawn or evening, day or night;—
Clinging as a constant treasure,—
Chirping with a cheerious measure,—
Wholly to my uncle's pleasure
    (Though his shoes were far too tight).

VI.

So for three and forty winters,
Till his shoes were worn to splinters,

All those hills he wander'd o'er,—
Sometimes silent ;—sometimes yelling ;—
Till he came to Borley-Melling,

Near his old ancestral dwelling
    (But his shoes were far too tight).

VII.

On a little heap of Barley
Died my agèd Uncle Arly,
    And they buried him one night ;—
Close beside the leafy thicket ;—
There,—his hat and Railway-Ticket ;—
There,—his ever-faithful Cricket
    (But his shoes were far too tight).

CPSIA information can be obtained at www.ICGtesting.com
Printed in the USA
LVOW09s1827180716

496773LV00010B/441/P